DEATH BY POETRY

MELANIE McCURDIE

Copyright © 2015 Melanie McCurdie
July 15, 2015
All rights reserved.

ISBN-13: 978-1515055563
ISBN-10: 1515055566

All Rights Reserved. No part of this publication may be reproduced, stored in a retrieval system, or transmitted, in any form or in any means – by electronic, mechanical, photocopying, recording or otherwise – without prior written permission.

Any names or characters, businesses, events or incidents, are fictitious. Any resemblance to actual persons, living or dead, or actual events is purely coincidental.

TABLE OF CONTENTS

Section A	1
Section B & C	12
Section D	18
Section E – H	27
Section I – L	40
Section M	50
Section P – R	65
Section S	74
Section T	88
Section U – Y	102

Poetry. Beautiful words, song lyrics, humorous limericks, it all counts. Long used to speak ones heart and let's be frank, woo the opposite sex, it comes in every genre, from vicious and bloody to heart wrenchingly eloquent and anything in between.

It is also an expression of one's heart and soul, of their pain or passion, of immediate inspiration or remembered events. Sometimes it's nothing more than the equivalent of a creative tantrum. An outburst.

It is meant to make you feel, either through eloquence or honesty, or simply just because someone's words resonate with you. And in that moment we find a new perspective or a kinship, or perhaps just a joyful place to lose yourself for a while.

As you make your way through these pages, you will find may such outbursts and tantrums, some are bloody, and some are not. My only hope is that you find some common thread that will take you further along your own path.

M. McCurdie

A

A ROMANTIC'S DREAM

The skulls flicker
Glow, dancing, wavering flames
Illuminating the white rose petals that litter the path
Lighting the way up the stairs

The chilly clink of my keys hitting the polished surface
Of the small table at the door sets my nerves on edge,
Too loud in the silence
Much like my heart pounding in my ears

The scent of the heavily perfumed rose petals,
Cloying, delicious and wrong
I climb the stairs in the dark and hesitate with my throat closing
The hallway is lined with skulls of a human kind,
Taper candles jammed into crudely bored holes

Ahead, the door to my bedroom stands ajar
My sanctuary breached, I am enraged, fear forgotten
Fly in fury, I cross the threshold and am lost to the beauty
A romantic's dream, perfectly executed
Expertly prepared for pleasure
It seemed I was a lucky girl
·There is one problem and it leaves me cold
I don't have a boyfriend
And I live alone

ANELIESE

Come play with me!!

The ocean cried
And tossed the small boat to and fro
The old man fraught with pride
Struggled and fought
Barely alive
Voice rising and falling
To the invisible man at his side
As the ocean bubbled and waved
In his faith began to confide
Praying to God to save him

God of the Sea, Poseidon, He
Laughed at the pleas so uttered
Trident in hand, he roiled the sea
Dove the scow deep, filled her with water
Held her there with no chance to flee
Then brought her up, let her draw air
Kissed her lips and sent her to the quay
Her half drowned passenger in tow

Along the sandy shoreline,
Night broken by the dawn
The scow came to a shuddering settle
Weather beaten and withdrawn
The passenger stumbled ashore
The place blanketed in unfamiliar briny mist

His lungs threatened to freeze
No friendly faces came to his rescue
Until into view came Aneliese

Cloak'd though she was, darkness surrounded
Her long dark hair tangled in the breeze
He knows each movement like his own heartbeat
Closer, dress rustling, comes Aneliese

Poseidon, His waves sound louder than before
An angry rushing like wind in his ears
Suddenly faces appear at the doors
Lanterns brighten the insistent gloom
In the light his mind begins to implore
His Aneliese, extrinsic beauty, dead, rotted
Horrified screams, beautiful no more

Mind gibbering he falls and flails
Voice barely piercing fear muffled ears
The mist echoes back terrified wails
Sharp as seabirds calls in the night
And a chuckle hard as nails
Cuts the sound like a knife
Faces gloomy fade behind the veil
Lights give back the darkness
How would I know the shadowy details?
Dead men tell no lies

ANGEL

Angel I am not.

It's just your angle of reflection
A momentary human disconnection
You caught me in a moment
Of unselfconscious distraction
Internal sunshine creates
A flexion connection
I was lost in internal dissection
Of my own imperfections
My own swan song tuneless
I got lost in introspection

Now think what you will
A predilection of distraction
The eternal equations battle
Resurrection or rejection
We fight the implication of perfection
Mirrors lie all the time
And beauty is but an advection
A pretty painted masque
Just means to ply the nature of attraction
With no intent to learn what lies inside

ANGEL IN MY POCKET

With hands clasped to my chest as though in death

Upright and walking, holding tight a tiny heart
Angel from my Pocket fights
Insisting to be let alone
Put back in his rightful place as conscience

I give you adulation, Angel
A pat on the back for a job well done
And now I stuff you, wings and all
Into a slingshot aimed at the Heavens
I release you of your bonds to me

Launch you at the sky
Shoot you straight back to where you came from
Today I do not need an Angel in my Pocket
When the Devil on my shoulder will do just fine

ANGELS/DEMONS

I make no plans or designs to show my true nature
If you forgive the cliché, what lies inside?
Few have seen it, even the shadow on the wall
Some have experienced it...teeth, claws and all

It's not pretty, the cobwebs and dust
Keep it at bay, with the booby-traps and mental duct tape
I've strung it like streamers
– Hither and yon – with no rhyme or reason

I could go on, but the point is thus
I've kept it caged – leashed with barbed wire, shackles and chains
If it's out, and you've been bitten, it's not my affair
What idiot willingly sticks his hand onto the Sharks mouth
and expects it to tickle?

The bars are rusting, wearing quite thin;
I've built them up, welded and such
And plied It with gin so I could work in relative safety,
Though I have lost an eye and sport lovely scarred
Scratches that never really heal
I hope the new cage comes soon
The dusty rusted flakes keep falling like bloody raindrops to the floor

Bloody raindrops to the floor

Bloody raindrops on the floor
An angel at the door
She shines like the Devil
In cut-off blue jeans

The beast gives a roar
Angel screams encore!
Her legs go forever in those
Cut-off blue jeans

I think I've lost my mind
It happens all the time
But the angel sits on my lap
Her body on fire inside those
Those.....

I know I've gone insane
It's evident, just plain
I'm being fucked by an angel
In cut-off blue jeans

My body is on fire
Taken higher, then higher
And leave my calling card inside
The angel in cut-off blue jeans

Her smile is poetic
Innocent, pathetic
That is no angel
In cut-off blue jeans

The beast gives a howl
A clattering, a scowl
It pounces oh its meal
In cut-off blue jeans

She screams like a banshee
Vibrating on the floor and she
Is quiet as she is entered
It becomes the monster
In cut-off blue jean

AN ODE TO INSPIRATION

Truly so, Muse
The bon mot escapes my brittle mind
Slithery thing that it is,
creeping and cavorting in the shadowy recesses
Dancing in the darkness in time to my cuckoo clock heart
La passionnante pas de deux with Inspiration,
While It loves me still

Thy acerbic tongue tempered
Lightened and enlightened
It speaks a language of blooms and blasphemy
Poisonous posies rival the reddest rose
Oh thou beastly demon

My heart quivers in my breast
Thy visions paint love upon my brow
Leaving only breathless frisson
And an ache I cannot slake

AN UNEXPECTED GIFT

Prey, I watch as they slumber
Silly, frilly, meatsacks
You, the naive and innocent
Cataclysm will touch you, ravage
Harvest calls, time to reap!
Obsiquitious, you shall be
Paroxysms of delight
An unexpected gift, door unlocked
Their skulls split, splattering blood hither and yon
Hold no remorse, say goodbye.

ARE YOU AWAKE?

Woman!

Get off your high horse and
Pull your head from the clouds

Wake the fuck up

You wield your words like a child
With a newfound weapon
Swinging them hither and yon
Swiping at anyone who comes close
And injuring only yourself.

I am here to tell you no one cares
About the petty high school bullshit
This is not a stage so cut the drama

It's boring, it makes you look gauche and
I have no time to be drawn into the
Debacle you find yourself in at your own doing

I have no interest in a kerfuffle
Participating in your fool's errand
This is not a game you will win
Do what you will, it's your own choice
Just take a look around you for once

YOU hold the key to the kingdom
You are the only one who can change it

Are you awake yet?

B & C

BEAUTIFUL LIE

It's beautiful on the surface
It shines, calls, sings your name
Allures you,
Pulling you in with
The crook of a finger

A dancer full of staggering grace
It stumbles and falls
Rises and soars
Seductress in rose coloured glasses

It darkles, cavorts
Mesmerizing you into believing all is perfection
Until you open your eyes
To find you are being burned alive

Under the thin veil it ripples like water
Dipping your fingers in
You don't see the flesh
Splitting away from your bones

Cleaved from within
Bites deeply with poisonous teeth
Dripping it's venom into your wounds
Where it stirs and boils as it numbs your soul

The song it sings is noxious and vile
It screams beauty but gives only
Pain and torture
Sweet suffering
Love

BURNING

Let's throw stones
Hard as you can, into the water
Watch the impact,
The splash is blood spray
You killed it
Did it feel good? Enjoy it?

.

Do it again
Cause the ripples that distort the reflection
The cold clear sky
The slight mist on the surface
Make it ugly

Do it again

Again

AGAIN, DO IT AGAIN

Scream, Curse the sky
Reach a level of profanity
Never experienced before

Throw your rage to the river
Let it drown
Watch it drown
Do Nothing
Let it die

BUT FOR THE CHILL

You touched me
your feather like caress raining chill upon my flesh
I feel the pressure of your fingertips
The cold passing of your palm against my cheek
Gently turning my head, your breath on my neck
I resist, these are not my memories
It's wrong to watch the life of another
To feel those moments of passion
It feels right, as a deep ache finally fulfilled

I taste the waxy flavour of chapstick
The salt of the sea on your lips
The fading mint of the gum you'd been chewing
I crave, yearn, Your touch is real
As real as the arm around me
Pressed around the small of my back
A hand wrapped in my hair
The teeth at my throat, biting, gently

I give over to it, surrender my will
Allow it to overtake me
Devouring, it grows claws, its talons puncturing my back
As its hardness invades my body
Pleasure and Pain
Gasping breathless delight
Icy discharge freezes my insides, warming them, then
Fading away as if a dream

But for the chill

BRUISES HEAL

Perfunctory kisses and loveless touches
Use my body and ignore my mind
Pleasures wrought and brought
Climax rushed and heartless
Once you told me pretty words
Without belittling and making me feel small
Like a last resort, some faceless vessel
I meant something then
Once my body was your playground
Now you fuck me and roll away
Leave me cold and heartsick

I feel like a kept whore
Sometimes in the night
Alone in our bed, beside you
Just wanting to be held as the tears start to flow
I drift to sleep hugging my pillow
To my chest, the only comfort I have
And wish that your fists would lash
Instead the torturous indifference
Because words sting forever

And eventually bruises heal

CLEAR

Do I appear stupid to you?

Some poor little fool who doesn't know her ass from her elbow?
I'm not
I see so much more than you give credit for
Cursed with intuitive logic
I see your patterns light up like neon lights
A möbius loop of deceit and prose
How many can be stacked one atop the other until it falls apart?
The center cannot hold if it's built on nothing

Until you, I had no belief in vampires
I had no need for creatures when I am surrounded by monsters

Manifesto by malicious intent
Methods employed to suck the life and love
From my lips and fingertips
Bent on your own pleasure & destruction

Fuck you
I revoke my invitation
I take it back
Slam the door and burn it down
There is no room left at the Inn

D

DANDELION FLUFF

A shooting star across the black
Make a wish you bid me
I close my eyes and say I wish I could
Stay with you forever in this bed of leaves
Under darkened skies
The midnight creatures rustling around us
Eerie footsteps pass us by
While dandelion fluff
Floats above my head from the seeds you blow
a dusty halo say you and I laugh
for my dark angel you say and I smile,
At the sun in your eyes
All that is perfection is right in this moment
As I lay with you in this bed of leaves

DAYDREAM

Oh what you do to me
Driving me out to rage in the rain,
The heavens pelting and hurling stinging needles
Soaking my cigarette, its tip fizzling in the damp

O fury, my constant companion
That you never abandon me
A devilish threesome, temptation
You draw me to the brink

From Walking the Path to owning it, slicing and dicing
Thrusting and twisting my blade
Scythe, talons, teeth
As the coyotes yip yip in the distance
On the other side of the fence
Their mouths full of lethal daggers
Glistening in the wet reflections
Eyes red and rabid, foaming
Nightmares or cuddly puppies

A scream rends the air
Bends the air, disrupts the bats in the trees,
How they flutter like furry butterflies
Stark against the moon

Scream, scream again
Pealing like a siren
Red hot icepick to my brain
I drive it into my eye
Scrambling the membrane

It's insane
Thrust, swirl, baked mind
It cooks on the tip

Howl, broken voice
Shattered and singing
A horribly beautiful aria
Bubble, gurgle
Choke on your blood
Air screaming from the hole
I made in your chest

Lick your lips, your tears
Suck the crimson fluid from your tongue
Drink you, drain you dry
Breathe you

You taste like spring
Green and bourgeoning death
Treacle pie with bloodsauce
You taste like new love
Fear and lust
Cinnamon and honey
Reverie broken
The rain stopped
So did he

DEAL WITH THE DEVIL

Would you make a deal with the Devil
Knowing how He speaks half-truths?

Would you listen as He spun a fantastic story,
Filled with vague promises and pretty words all designed
In hopes you may crumple your soul like discarded thoughts
Throw it all away for your heart's desire?

I don't want to play these foolish games
To listen to attempted, poisonous dénouements in my darkest time
Desiccated sentiments that mean nothing
They fall like sloughed skin from lips riddled in lies

Belief no more, fallen on deaf ears
They cannot penetrate my frozen heart

Begone from my sight, Demon, plague me no more
Once I believed, until your true colours shone

DELUGE

The touch of your hand
On my face, tilting so that I see you
There the passion lies
The sensation makes me want to live
Love, a thousand times over

The taste of your lips, warm
Won over in your arms,
A sweet surrender, forfeit battles
My fight stolen in electric combat,
It burns me alive inside

Inferno, your nearness is desire
To live immortal in your embrace
Knowing that your soul is an oasis
And a playground for mine
I know where happiness resides

Being with you makes me want to live
The shortness of time compounds
Time flows forward, inevitably
My heart grows ever fonder
Bittersweet and true

Please don't touch me that way
The touch of your hand
The taste of your lips
Knowing that your soul is an oasis
The knowledge makes me want to die

DRAW

You look at me as though I am crazy
When I laugh at your professions
And look away
Anywhere but caught in your ocular embrace
Why, you ask and block my stare
Turn my gaze, and draw me in
Draw a tear, draw another
Draw a smile and fetch a sigh
Knowing I will never understand
Yet again my hands gloved in cruor
What it is that is so interesting, to men,
That they cannot resist a Monste

E – H

EVERY DAY

I come every day
bringing flowers and snippets of bad poetry in an attempt to woo

I come every day
and stand beneath the ladder her bare feet rest on,
watching the wind in her hair

I come every day
and scream at her while brandishing my fist and she turns away

I come every day
and sit by the tree to watch the flesh fall from her bones
And regret

FIRE

Fire
Feel it lick at the edges
My skin a fury
The internal debate
Exquisite pain as I burn

BURN

Eyes the igniter
Surface reflecting a deeper yearning
A blowtorch to the chill, the knowing
Cravings intensify, temptation tremors
They double, treble
Blown apart as they depart
None stand before strength
Of mind, as it faces desire
I weep in its presence
Warm to the touch, it incinerates
It destroys as it adores
Endures, never absent
Heart blackened, iridescent as the raven's wing,
It joyfully roars, freedom rings
I drift to peaceful, peaceable dreams
Safe in the knowledge
I can overcome,
Even filled with flames
I smoulder as I turn to ash

GOTTA LIGHT?

The flame lights up the shadow thrown by
His rakishly cocked fedora as he lights his cigarette
Trench coat firmly belted, the collar up at the back
"Here's looking at you schweetheart" in a bad Bogey imitation
And I smile, and shake my head,
Looking away from the intensity of his dark eyes

Somethings don't change, I think,
Ever the joker, even when it ended

"So you're still carrying a torch for her?"

I raise my eyes, my eyebrow as well
Meeting a serious expression that staggers the breath in my chest
He holds out his hand, the lines in his palm still the same,
The tattoo on his wrist, the zipper, oh how we laughed
And I hesitate, it hurt the last time
I don't want to be hurt again

His eyes, those damnable eyes
His arms, around me, hand on my neck
Kisses that scream I missed you
I love you
Never leave again

"So you're still carrying a torch for her?"

I smile into his face in momentary hesitation

"Gotta light?"

HITTING HOME

You couldn't help yourself, could you?

Just had to have it, ply and plead
Poetry and promises
Pretty words meant to crack veneer
Like stones on a frozen pond
Just kept hammering it home

It hit home, believe it
Like a punch in the solar plexus or a knee in the box
Still standing, though bleeding
Still breathing, despite the arrows

You couldn't help yourself.

I say its bullshit, lying to your heart so you can lie to mine
Spreading lye on the memories that mean something to me
It makes it ugly and I see that enough
In the mirror each morning

Reality bites, hard
And it's coming fast
Maybe then it'll hit home for you too

HOME FIRES BURNING

Once I was Home.
I was home to my family
My body housed life and suffered death
I lay in solitude, listening to him breath
Listening to the quiet ticking of the clock on the wall.

It was Tuesday, late when
He staggered to our bed still wearing that damned fedora
And her perfume and nothing else
I was lonely, and miserable that night in the dark, my eyes closed,
Riding the waves of pleasure and smelling her all over him
I felt so small

My fingers tracing the scratches she left behind
When he came, it was inside me
It scalded like my tears when he rolled away,
and murmured her name as he drifted to sleep.

I lay alone, last Tuesday
Shivering in the lightless room in effort to be silent while he snores
Mourning and knowing that I didn't want him
I just wanted contact
I needed to be warm
To feel something other than the numb cold
Always stuck struggling with the endless knowledge that he was
elsewhere, often while I was trapped here

It is Tuesday, evening
I pace the gleaming wooden floors

Eyes on the clock on the mantel
Eyes on the front door

I made this hell a home
No children to fill the empty hallways
The long empty days last forever and when night falls the cobwebs

Flutter and the Ghosts dance through the in-between spaces
Knocking on the walls and doors
Sometimes they cast shadows on the glass

They become people again with the endless chatter
Endless opinions
Endless questions
Unable to grasp my sorrow

So today I hid in the darkened parlour
Choosing to stop the insistent fight and let my sanity skip and slip
I drank champagne and ate oranges
Danced barefoot on the thorny line where my sanity capered and
Cried until I laughed

I'm still laughing as he begs and pleads from the bed
Where I said my last goodbye
Painted his thoughts with my tongue, carved my name into his flesh
When he filled me with his tainted seed

The air is heavy with the scent of fire, the echoes of screams ringing
Outside the sirens wail and he burns in our bed
Thrashing and writhing
Speaking in tongues

I watch him struggle and finger the stem of my champagne glass
The weight of my other too much to bear
But I lift it anyway and place it against the supple shelf
Under my chin in thought and reflection
And pull the trigger with a smile

HONEYED AGONY

The thoughts keep swirling around in my brain
A demented mind movie behind my eyes
Torture and sweetness
They make me want to howl
Honeyed agony
Kill me now
Bliss
Anguish

Feign indifference
It's turned to ice
Burning inside
Can't melt the shell no matter how hot the flame burns

It was for me
Harshly, it was
Now muzzled and bound
Propriety for Propriety's sake
Clipped wings, an eagle can't soar
I fucking hate it
Swallow it back
Choke it down
Weep

Over and over, bloody droplets
From a slow leak, slice
Drowning in the air
I want to scream
I need to rage

I want to plunge

The Knife and Kill it
Put it to rest
Hold it close

Cherish and adore
Loathe to Love
Love

Stupid Heart
Just die already

Big girls don't cry
Its weakness, and it's useless
Wasted emotion
Precious fluids
It's human
I don't want to be anymore.

HORIZON

up and down
up and down
the swells make my head explode
makes my heart ache in sympathy
for my stomach, my ears

look for the horizon
look to the horizon
there is no shore
only water, and the horizon

Burning alive, i want water
i have no water, surrounded by it and not a drop to drink

There is another, we are the last
not survivors, we won't unless help comes
lost in the vastness, we will die here
oh i don't want to be sick again
my eyes leaking valuable fluids

it hurts and i want to die
i don't want to die

squeeze my eyes shut
hallucination
it has to be

the other looks different to me now

shivering in my skin, ripples of chill
enclosed in the sun's deathrays

I need water
the other stares at me mouth slightly open

eyes dead in their watchfulness
i feel like food
god help me
not food, alone

I'm alone, surrounded by water
the horizon, just water and the horizon

and the sun, oh burning me
precious fluid lies stagnating in the other
dying with each second
it would slake the thirst
my heart refuses
the body demands

so far to go
too far
as my body moves of its own accord
eyes on the fever cooling liquids
strength and survival, strength
and survival

it gushes out after the cut
after the small blade I pried
from the others fingers

its water

its water
believe that it's water

i press my lips against the cut
sucking in deep the red
the blood

the water
its just water
please god
its just water

how long have i been here?
how many days
hours
minutes
seem like days
the horizon is on fire
the other has gone
a feast for the beasts

i can't
please god i can't
not anymore
pry the cup from my lips
be kind to this sinner
non believer
take me home

its day again
how many days
i remember the hole

gaping black hole

screaming
killing there was killing
blood and screaming
fists teeth lifeboats gone
left
just left by everyone
only we two
the other and me we found this
and jumped and floated
on the bubbling sea vomit
as the air from our vessel exploded
to the surface and pushed
shoved us out further
and now there is me

look to the horizon
look for the horizon

surrounded by water
and not a drop to drink

pray to god
prey to the Other
beg plead

please

please

take me

i can't

my skin hurts
my teeth hurt
my mind hurts

up and down
up and down

burning

i need water

surrounded by water

no shore

the horizon
the horizon

look to the horizon

horizon

home

I – L

I LIE HERE

i lie here
day after day, night after night
night is better
the small creatures feed me
so that I can maintain the last vestiges of life I cling to

i lie here
day after day, night after night
when the rain comes and fills my empty eyes devoid of emotion but
for sadness - it holds me here

i lie here
day after day, night after night
the warmth of the day reminds me of the warmth of his hand
the smoothness of his palm against my cheek

i lie here
day after day, night after night
In the comforting darkness
Hearing him tell me close your eyes and feel, FEEL
and I'd feel him so close, his scent still lingers on my tongue

i lie here
day after day, night after night
Waiting, for moments
for decades, forever
he said he'd come back

INDULGE-DENY

A discussion of the Consciousness'

Behold, thine eyes are a wonder

Have another joint

I cry love to your ears

Do you really buy that crap?

To touch, to hold, to drink your darkness is heaven

That means I want to fuck you

Yes. It does. Now bend over.

Fin

IN THIS PLACE

Laying here feeling nothing
Except the hook twisting and turning in my guts
In the dark few hours on my own
I'm afraid and wondering
If I run, what's the danger
I don't want to be in pieces
To be in this place
The sterility makes me nauseous
I stand and fall
With my belly screaming
I miss you and I'm scared
So out of contact
No one to talk to that understands
I want to feel safe and warm
No agony and fear
But you're not here
Fast moving blurs smother me
In incoherent chatter
My tears drying in the breeze they create
The clock just rushes forward
The needle brings blackness
I close my eyes and try to forget
I'm alone.

JUDGE AND HANGMAN'S JURY

Listen

Don't talk to me like you know
You don't know anything
Not about me. Not about my life.
And not about then.

Don't beg me to speak and then admonish my tale
Asking inane and stupid questions
Whose answers still terrify

Still, you claim you understand
In a manner most haughty
Under the guise of concern

I know with no doubt, fragile thing
You'd never live through it yourself

Blindness, is Judge and Hangman's Jury
The judgment isn't it your words but in how you say them

So when again you ask why I'm still here
Instead of giving in, then
For the millionth time I say

I did.
Often.
And still I breathe.

LEGION

He says

There's something
In the corner
Under a sheet
that I don't like.

I tell him
It's a work in progress
It's not ready
Leave it alone
For now

I tell him
It bites
Its seethes
It giggles
Maniacally

He says
It's not alive
It can't be
I don't like it
Make it stop

I tell him
It's got claws
Eyes drip blood

It drools venom

I made it
Its mine
It scares me
He says
It's wrong
Not natural, not right
Get rid of it
Destroy it

I tell him
But I love it

I lift the sheet
It grabs him
And giggles
Sucking his eyes
From his face
Excising life

I tell him
You can't see it
It is perfect
It is sublime
It is destruction
It is apocalypse
Its name is Legion
I'm not ready to unleash it
Yet

LOVE FALLS

When Love falls before you
Heart bloodied and embattled
Hands held up in supplication
Wings once glorious tattered and torn
Would you gather it to your breast
Envelop and immerse it
Gently caressing its soul with words soft as a kiss

Would you whisper "stay"
Should it struggle to leave
Out of injurious fear
If it cried please let me go
Should it bite, would you hold it
Tighter against your own heart
Let it scream rage in tears

Would you turn it away
Held at arms length, would you resist
Would you laugh at it's its need, disgusted
Desire unfulfilled
Would you accept it to you a gift in plain sight
A Treasure to cherish
Given of free will
What will you do
When Love falls before you

LULLABY, BABY GOODNIGHT

Fell asleep to the sounds of gunfire
In the arms of chilly concrete
Screaming goes on in her head
Alone in the ruins of a normal life
A four-year old Ancient weeps

She knows no life different
But dreams of so much more
Things she sees only in dreams
A home, a warm meal, a family
In her sleep the angel smiles

Lullaby,
Lullaby, baby goodnight

You are not the only ones who feel you have nothing
Look closer and see
Reach deep inside and find your humanity
It's the only way we can survive

It's your lullaby
Lullaby, baby goodnight

Our lives are so easy
Struggle is heavenly to those with nothing
Yet we complain over small insignificant things
It's time to wake up and smell the reality

Take a good look around you and visualize
Open your eyes and see

Lullaby,
Lullaby, baby goodnight

She fell to bed exhausted to the sound of his breathing
Struggling to breathe and smile leaves her drained
Deep in the night she lies awake wondering and
Worrying about the fate of her family
How they will go on when she's gone

Misery loves company yet she's alone
Unable to fight it she escapes to the darkness
Cutting her skin she sees the light
In relief the angel smiles

It's your lullaby
Lullaby, baby goodnight

You are not the only ones who feel you have nothing
Look closer and see
Reach deep inside and find your humanity
It's the only way we can survive

Lullaby
Lullaby, baby goodnight

Our lives are so easy
Struggle is agony to those in despair
Yet we complain over small insignificant things
It's time to wake up and smell the reality
Take a good look around you and visualize
Open your eyes and see

Lullaby, baby goodnight
It's your lullaby
Baby Good Night

M

MAMA SAYS

Mama says

I must be a good girl
and stay here
and be quiet.

Mama says

Learn your books
and learn your prayers
and be quiet

Mama says it's important

She touches my hair a
and smiles into my eyes
and calls me her good quiet girl

Mama says

Stop it child
Slaps me on my cheek
Then kisses the hot place when I start to cry

Mama says

You are a daemon
People are afraid of you
They don't understand

Mama says

My beautiful quiet girl
Learn your books
Learn your prayers

Mama says

I can't
You mustn't
And smiles in a scary way

Mama says
Nothing

Mama left me

Her blood is on the floor
On the door.
On the ceiling.
On the walls

Papa says

GET THEE BEHIND ME SATAN

Staring at me with his eyes all wide
Like the preacher Mama brought
To teach me to be Godly

Papa says

I am not your father

Your mother fucked the Devil
You are a plight on the Earth

Papa says he hates me

Papa says

Go back to hell
and hurts me with his knife
and makes me bleed

Papa says

Bad words that hurt me more
When I hold my red fingers up
and he laughs

Papa says

It's a lie, you are not human
I'll prove it
Papa opens the front door

Papa says

There is your father
Papa points to the porch

The Dark Man waits
Papa says

Take her
and the Dark Man stands and his eyes glow like mine

Papa screams

The Dark Man says
Come Child
Mama says

MEMOIR

I sit at the airport
Awaiting the flight
That will take me away
You're out of touch and I'm out of time

The simplest words I couldn't say
I dared not speak its name
Refusing to give it its final voice
For giving it air allows it to grow

Instead, I left a note, where I hoped you would find it
It holds so much of my soul
So much of my self-worth
Is tied up in desire
My heart is broken
Stuck on that word
That I couldn't articulate

I couldn't tell you when I would hear your voice
Afraid of what might be found
It's lodged in my throat
Choking as it clings
Nearly begging to be held back
My tears fall my flight is called
Knowing you found it
My final word

Goodbye

MINDLESS

My ass is wet from sitting on
Rain soaked stairs, the carpeting
Musty and in need of change
Because I'm too fucking lazy
To stand as I'm pelted in the eyes
With raindrops from heaven
That feel like boulders

In my elevated state of mind
I'm imagining a sun filled destination
Where tequila flows like water
And cigarettes are not being shot
Out of your hands with laser cannons
Because everybody smokes
And nobody cares

A place where my wandering mind
Can caress the endless blue horizon
Like the habitual voyeur I am
Watch as it changes colours like clothing
With no worries or care just mindless
Not that I do care
Because I don't about much

Except my ass being wet
On these stairs in the rain

MIRROR SHOWS

You speak no words
And tell me I'm beautiful with your eyes
Becoming exasperated when I avert my gaze
I know in your mind I am as you say and
It pleases me and confuses when you demand to know why
Every time I crack wise or deflect, can I not just accept?
I just don't know how to explain to you that
What you see is not what the mirror shows
You say beauty, but all I see
Are scars and haunted eyes

MISERY LOVES COMPANY

I first saw her reflection
In the shop window of that absurd little doll store
The one on 5th and Main?

Tragically gorgeous in that B Movie kind of way
I couldn't take my eyes from her curves and edges
The porcelain perfection of her complexion
And those lips. Full and pouty
Red in that almost garish porn star way
On her it was fresh cherries of the tree
I was willing to bet they tasted as good

And there I stood
Stunned into silence with my cock at full mast
Holding a half-naked children's toy in my hand
It felt like I was smiling but likely I was leering
And be goddamned if she didn't return my lustful stare
And flick her tongue out like some living thing
And taste the right of the lollipop she'd been playing with
Before pushing it slowly between her wet looking lips
Never dropped her eyes

I thought I had died, just then
When she smiled at me
And called me forward with one black tipped finger
And I came. And went to her with my cheeks burningThe front of
my jeans beginning to show a dark spot
I wanted to run but she put her hand **THERE**
Put her mouth on mine and I was sure I was in hell

When the shopkeeper cleared his throat
And she stopped licking my teeth
To look at him, hand squeezing my tortured dick
Nodded and released me,
Saying *come see me if you want company*.
The man snickered and finally guffawed
Before staring me soberly in the eyes
Take an old man's advice, he said
Lighting his match with a worn fingernail
And holding it to his home rolled cigarette
She loves company. Don't be her next conquest.

I handed him the doll I'd ceased fondling
Thanking him for his sage advice and his time
Turning, I saw the most amazing thing
Full sized dolls, dressed in 50's clothing
So realistic I laughed in spite of myself
And the Shopkeep said
Remember what I said.

I didn't listen, of course
And followed her home in my old green pickup
Watch her struggle with her playthings
Cursing and spitting vile and deviant admonishment
It shocked me, and intrigued me
So I jumped out of my truck
And ran to her rescue and she smiled
Kissing me full on my mouth and
pressing her firm breasts to my chest

All the while hearing the shopkeeper's raspy words
I wondered about how much company she kept
I wondered what her name was
I wondered how **HE** knew
As I stepped through her front door

That was forever ago
Before I found that I loved her
My captor, my demon, my wife

And my questions were answered
In more detail than I care to remember
Mustn't frown! She wants smiling happy people
My father in law you have met, briefly
You really don't want to make his acquaintance
Or hers, because it's like Pops, the Shopkeeper says, my wife,
Misery, Loves company.

MISUNDERSTOOD

I wonder sometimes
If you see me as human
Or see me at all

Dismissing my request
In a joking manner, you say
You know I can't stay
With a shake of your head
As you walk away, turning your back
You're just insatiable
It can wait

I roll over to hide
My ache and tears
Because that's not the reason at all
I just need you near

You stop in the doorway
Tell me you love me
And leave me lonely, alone

MOONLIGHT

You taste like moonlight and blood
Just like the night we met,
In the forest
Where we walked hand in hand
And you told me all the secrets I longed to hear
With the crickets playing a symphony
To the percussion of the darkness
That ebbed and flowed around us.
Centuries ago, yesterday
My life became forfeit
My mundane existence stolen
Volunteered, the slaughter ahead enticing
You laid me down and loved me
Imbibed me, and you tasted like moonlight

MURDER OF ONE

Merlot on white
The shadows pulse and throb
There's blood on the tombstones

We are in the non-time here, the minutes frozen
The world awash with in silver light
All blues, and blackness

Flying against the moon the carrion birds call
Their black wings a flutter of darkness
A shadow crossing the pale beauty's face

I am a murder of one, stalking the night
Preying in the shadows, lying in wait
While the Knowledged Ones cavort and shriek

Ruckus, raucous, their rusty serenade rising and falling
Casting their spells of wonder and terror, naked, glistening
In languages lost, she screams steadily
Rending the air with her madness

MYTH

The Heart
We speak of it being sensitive
Fragile, tender and soft but it's not

How could it be when we take a knife to it over and over again?
Bleed out every time the membrane is breached
And still you open that door
Hoping against hope that this time is different, that the words
spoken are real; that you found someone to believe in you
Only to have those dreams dashed on the rocks

The atrocities we visit on our emotional center
Should leave us ashamed, driven to be kinder
It doesn't, for we cause harm everyday
In love, we hold it high, cupped in our palms

We offer it as sacrifice,
It sings songs of fairy tales and dark delights
But none of it is reality, a pipe dream
We rip off the Handle with Care labels
Play the game until the pain begins and you are left
Only the heartache, heartbreak is inevitable
Because we are too stupid to learn

The Heart
The only organ that can be crushed, shattered, maimed
Pierced and burned from within and still it beats when you'd rather
Lie down in the Clearing and Die
Insisting on spouting its inspired bullshit
It beats on and on,
Stupid Heart

P – R

PARADISE FOUND

Once there was joy
Enraptured in life
Rejoiced in the darkness

A paradise found

Where all things were possible and are
To be what you wish Dream it, it's true
Build a world where everything is shiny and new
Or the world of old
Where warriors roamed protecting fair maidens
From terrors unknown

A land of the lost with Giants and Gods
Monsters walked the Earth
Roaring their dominance over all
Perhaps our own world
Where droplets of inspiration fall from the fingertips
Of one just awakened
A mind that lay dormant now lost in its thoughts
Jolted alive, brought to with a shock

The little things are what matters most
The love of a friend
The taste of spring
The smile that touches
The lips of a lover
The scent of the rain
The first floral blooms
The sight of the stars

Or just the full moon

Paradise found

It was there all along
Just open your eyes
Open your heart
See the small things
Know what they are
Nuggets of gold
Worlds on a string
All that we are
All we can be
Living embodiments
Of Inspired moments

PERPLEXED

You look confused
You laughed
Sitting in your chair
Across the mellow wood table

Your words,
They perplex me
Astound me
They scare me
With the ease in which they
Slip through chinks in the armour

I am, I reply
Disintegrating resolve
Standing to walk away
It's simply not real

Your lips end the debate
Safe in your embrace
You whisper *but I do*

POLITICS AS I SEE IT

Talk
Talk
Talk
Threats
Death
Debate
Protests

More Talk
More Blather
More Action
Still more Talk
Still more Debate
Still more Protests
Still more Blather
Still more Action
Still more Threats

Death
Explosions
Death
Invasions
Death
Wars
Death
Bombs
Death

Bomb the fuck out of everyone that opposes you
Or die trying and take as many with you as you can

Kill everyone that crosses you
It doesn't matter the reason
Pick one Health Care, Human Rights, and Religious Freedoms
Soon there will be no one left to bomb,
maim, destroy or uproot

Then what?

The population is filled with different individuals
with differing morals and ideals
Sooner or later, the weapons will be pointed at you….
Isn't it easier to just co-exist?

QUIET TIME

I sit on this embankment that crawls with insects
It's our quiet time
Just listening
to the sound
of your voice
full of grave dirt
and maggots

Maggots

They boil from the wounds in your bloated body
Where it split after gasping for air
Where you surfaced, after breaking your bonds
Where you lodged in that fallen tree

Fallen Angel
Far from the place where we picnicked
Under a weeping birch on a blanket
Under the stars, you kissed me
Under the blanket you found me

Devious Devil
You grew fangs and claws
Screaming your pleasure and crying pain
Until I fucked you again with my knife
Leaving you hissing and screeching like a wildcat in heat
Your little death became the big dirt nap
and
so
I

Waited til just before dawn
weighted you down as best as I could and threw your naked body
over the bridge
Where the sign says Caution: Slippery When Wet
Your blonde hair streams like a glowing ribbon lighting your way
And your eyes begged me no as you hit the water and sank to the
bottom

But
you
were

NEVER CONTENT, you ball busting bitch
Never content to do as you should
Never content to just stay put
And you broke away, from where you'd be safe

I found you here when I came to escape
Those townie halfwits who giggled like hyenas
When I froze in the street, and

Saw you there
Saw you in your little red skirt
Saw your blonde hair gleaming
Saw your teasing smile at the rising in my jeans and
I knew
I knew you were waiting for me
I knew it was time
Now shhhh…
Wait your turn
It's our quiet time.

REAPER'S ENCHANTMENT

For years it glittered
The golden ring on her finger
A well-worn symbol of her love and devotion
In happier moments she wore it with pride,
content in her emotional inertia
Glad to have a warm body to cuddle up with
Sometimes felt like a handcuff or a cage without bars
on the long lonely nights when she was alone and sleepless,
with everything she wanted within grasp
and unable to reach because she was chained
Still, she stayed with him for those many years.
The ring never left her finger, even when her heart had flown
She still loved on.

She doesn't know I'm here
Watching her stand over the casket with her shoulders shaking
and I love her more when she breaks, her slender well-curved body
shivering in grief. I've waited for her,
Watched her in pleasure
Watched her in pain
Watched her stare right through me Waited....
She slips the ring from her finger, holds it to her lips in silent prayer
Turns her head as my soul brushes the ceiling
and places it in his cold hand
Her tears drying on her cheeks, she smiles and catches my hear
When she reaches out and takes my hand

S

SAINTS OR SINNERS

Awake again, 3 am
I can't sleep anymore
Remembering your liar's touch
Leaves me broken on the floor

The mistake you tried to rectify
I still can't understand
And it still doesn't do much to clarify
Why you lied to me

We are all Sinners and Saints
Admit it or not it's still true
3 am is the darkest time
For Sinner or Saint, for you

The Devil's Daughter in lily white clothes
Your innocence is presupposed
Silver spoon baby, evil to the core
You left me shattered, on the floor

Are you really so cruel
Eyes such an allegory
Cold as ice, twice as devious
One day you will regret me

Your every move is a pantomime
Strategically planned to gain attention
Oh people can be so blind but
I know each of your secret intentions

It's the external battle that no one ever wins
But you my dear take the cake
I see the future in your lies
And forgetting me was your first mistake

We are all Sinners and Saints
Admit it or not it's still true
3 am is the darkest time
For Sinner or Saint, for you

You really are that cruel
Eyes such an allegory
Cold as ice, twice as devious
Are you Sinner or Saint?

SALVE

No
I replied
When you stood too close
Asking me to look at you
Your finger a spot of warmth
Under my chin, tilting my head

No.
I cried, eyes closed and moist
Your gentle request denied
But why? Your voice low
Betraying your thoughts
When I turned away
My arms wrapping around my body
An effort to hold the
Threatening shards of my broken heart together,
Duct tape of self-preservation

Because, I whisper, your embrace
A salve to my aching soul
I just got you out of my eyes
All I could see is you
If I look, you'll never leave
You said
I am home

SENSATION

Passion and laughter
Cotton candy
Handholding and movies
Sex on the beach
Champagne and strawberries
Dancing by moonlight
Long lasting stares
Smooth merlot
Salted caramel
Long hot tongue kisses
Filled and fulfilled
Sleepy snuggling
First smiles in the morning

All these things you are to me

SHEDDING SKIN

Wooden matches come alive
Paper roses weeping
Burst into fantastic flame

Just burn it away
Throw it away
Suffer like I suffer every day

Wood logs in a metal can
Doused in lighter fluid
A new life to begin

Burn away the I love you's
Burn away the love we made
Burn away everything you meant to me
Burn it away

Pages torn from an empty life
Crumpled, stuffed in crevices
This is how you left me, dying

Just burn it away
Throw it away
Suffer like I suffer every day

Burn away the nights
Driving hell-bent for freedom
Screaming live forever

Burn away the I love you's
Burn away the love we made
Burn away everything you meant to me
Just burn it away

Throw it away
Suffer like I suffer every day
Burn it away

Burn away the love you's
Burn away the love we made
Burn away everything you meant to me
Burn it away

SIGH

I am blind
Senses numbed
I feel nothing
And close my eyes
I'm alive again
Fire burning
Senses are singing
You are so near
I stumble forward
I fall into your arms
And am swept away
No words needed
I want
I need, love
The emotions, go unspoken
Blinking, I awaken
I'm aggrieved
And I cry
Not real, but real
Sleep claims me again
Aching inside

SLOW DANCE

Dressed in my best, casual
I don't care wear
I, the perpetual wallflower
Do what I do best

I decorate the bleachers
With all the other grapes dying on the vine
Some are small, grown sour and bitter
Others are soft and complacent
Nearly dead but clinging to hope
Still others, the rare ones
Firm and ripe for the picking
If the scales would fall from the eyes
Of the deliberately blinded
Those with their devotions to cliques and clubs
Snobs all the same
But no, we diligent few
Permanent, invisible dance décor
Sit and watch the barely moving mass
Slightly shifting to the beat

All these years and nothing has changed
Just older, in some cases, no wiser
Even the wallflowers are the same, those that remain
Some got married,
Produced more blandness to the population
Five, are gone, rest them
The memorials plastered amateurishly on the walls
The garish, whole-hearted sympathy makes them beautiful

One is now Nicole, rather than Nick
Shame really, to lose such…..
Passion in the Pit….though, she is stunning
Good Lord they are not playing that song
I may just vomit, maintain my control
And roll my eyes instead

I hear laughter and turn to a sight I'd forgotten
That glorious boy had become a man
I'm loathe to elevate him to God and
Leave him at Minor with room to advance
The smile, still the same, still makes me quiver
With its Devilish hunger and Gallant intent
How I laugh, my hair tickling my back
Head thrown back in hilarious dismay
When he said that he'd missed my laugh
Preferred it to watching me cry
That was sobering and a little worrisome
As I took in his voracious stare
Felt his teeth tear at my clothes
Moments before the lights went out

Girlish screams, churlish laughter, more than one lewd remark
Before I felt a hand on my waist, another over my mouth
I let him drag me away, let him move behind me
As he began whispering vile things in my ear
All while professing worshipful threats
For all these years he growls

All. These. Years
Each word punctuated by a thrust
Arousal evident against my ass

Some fucking reunion
Wouldn't you know it?
Shoulda, woulda, coulda
It didn't help. I got ready to fight
The world whirled, so did my head
Then I was in the arms of Adonis
Same devil with a different face
I began to recall details
That fiasco of a date, once time only
How soft his lips were on mine
His hand firmly on my breast

His mother
My father
Hell

That song
I hate that fucking song
And we are swaying, he is singing into my eyes, quietly
Slow dancing in streetlights
Falling in love

He falls on the ground
Blood bubbling from the corners of this mouth
Asking silently why, I stand over him, laughing, watching
He dies there gasping, like a fish out of water

Cold water washes sin away
Absolves my actions
Frees my soul

Back again, here I sit
I, the perpetual wallflower
Doing what I do best

SPECTRE

The eye of the storm is the center of the fire
Oxygen to feed the flames
He doesn't say much
Spectre in the shadows
Lingering, edges fluttering in and out of sight
I know what he wants and he can't have it
Not without a fight
Now as the sky bleeds
Darkness falls
Creatures shunned by the light play
I stand by the window
Hand on the glass
Over the reflection that grows brighter
And as I see him glance my way
Drifting towards the place of rest
I whirl about, anger flaring
Screaming my rage I point at him

"Dammit Grim, that Scythe is mine! Get your own!!"

SPINNING

You looked at me, and said
Can you give me reasons not to love you?
And I sighed and began to speak, for what seemed like hours.
You silenced me lips with your fingertip
Staring into my eyes, said,
Can you give me reasons to love you?
And I was speechless
I was speechless and you kissed me
Softer than eider down and with every ounce of strength you have
I was breathless and so were you as the night sky sparkled
The clouds and the wind were the breath of love and
We laid together under the stars
And lay together as you explained the heavens and
I, content to listen, encircled
The light from the stars
It takes aeons to shine
The ones who shine brightest, died long ago, perished
What we see are ghosts of the past, dancing above us, as we lay,
They are worlds you whisper, as
I fall asleep in your arms
And all the worlds stop spinning

T

TALK

She sits quietly staring at her hands
Lost in thought
Her fingers writhe like snakes
Entangled and ensnared
Caught in her lap - Caught in her eye

She sits quietly staring at her hands
Her thoughts writhe like snakes
Entangled, ensnared
Caught in the word-trap - Caught in her eyes

She sits quietly staring at her hands
Her heart writhes like snakes
Entangled, ensnared
Choking on the words - The ones caught in her eyes

She sits quietly staring at her hands
The thoughts, words unspoken
Cannot be articulated, enunciated

Fear holds her captive
The madness is taking hold

She sits quietly staring at her hands
Lost in thought
She speaks in silence
Not a word she will vocalize
Since I cut out her tongue

TINY DANCER

Tiny dancer
Undulates screaming
Enraptured. Incensed
In the bottle
I keep on the shelf
How she glows in the firelight
Long forgotten wings ablaze with ashes
A rage begotten demon
The acid drip of beautiful words
Fall from her bitch's tongue
In her mind, in my mind

I hear the cold-blooded murder
The lunacy whirlwind
She is the perfect beast
Completely cognizant, she freezes
Stares, gossamer feathers
Once midnight, now bloody
Calling me to sin. I resist her demands
And stand, the intricate weavings
The blanket I throw over the bottle

It does little to dampen the pulsating light,
But it does throw pretty patterns on the walls.

THE LITTLE THINGS

Little spills
Sit and stare
At the bottle

Little taste
Little waste
Guzzle it down
Feel it burn

Little ideas
Little thoughts
Big choices
Just stop

Little voices
Little screams
Small reminders
Of what could be

Little feelings
Little heart
Small losses
Where to start?

Little love
Little need
Small wants
Not necessary

Little cuts
Little bleeds
Tiny droplets
Don't hurt much

Little tears
Little pain
Small withdrawal
It means nothing

Little secrets
Little lies
Small regret
It is what it is

Little smiles
Little grin
Small shards
Cleave within

Little sigh
Little pang
Small sacrifice
Too much to gain

Little pieces
Little parts
Small bloodletting
Rage turns in

Little words
Little thoughts
Little everything
God its dark

THE LORD OF TEMPTATION

He's a sick bastard
Capering around waving
my cravings like a flag.

I hate him and adore him.
Cursing his existence and begging for more
I wonder if I could kill him.

Crime of passion.

Slice off his face like rubber cement from the table.
Cut out his cruel heart and squash it.
Slit his gizzard and dance in the entrails.

Cut his throat.

In cold blood is no problem.
My blood is never warm.

Humanity wails and whines,
insisting that it's not right
to end something that cannot help itself.

The Lord of Temptation lies dead on the floor

I couldn't help myself.

THE MESSAGE

The skulls waver in whispery rattles
Dead snapdragons along the white picket fence, speckled
Dusted here and there with a garish red that could only be real

I can hear her in there struggling,
fighting to breathe and survive me
I admire her commitment, truly I do
But it's all in vein, all over the floor...she lays living near the door

And I sit smoking another joint, bloody and naked
In plain sight of the surveillance camera
The one at the gas station across the street
Knowing full well it can see me, I spread my long legs wide
Exposing my intimate place to the world
and making good use of my fingers
Stroke myself off slow then fast,
bringing a sober and joyless orgasm flooding
A slight breeze in the face of gale winds,
euphoria and elevation reached
Legs slam shut, roach stored for later and I sigh

Inside, my lover awaits, bound to a chair
At his feet, as before a King she lays trying as she lays dying
His expression torn between lust and desire
Arousal evident as he squirms in his bonds
Horrified as I dispatch her quickly
and am engulfed in her sticky discharge
It tastes salty and hot, coating my face,
dripping thickly down my breasts

In his restraints, he became a beast,
Roaring in anger and mewling in pain
Groaning around the ball gag I straddle his lap
and sink his cock deep
Rocking my hips and scratching my nails across his chest,
It doesn't take long before he's ready

Growing larger still as he strains,
head thrown back and gag slick with spit
I slice his throat, the skin rolling back,
a secondary orgasm he cums blood
Open mouthed, splattering and gurgling

They'll find him there, till in his chair, still in his throes
Death and pleasure, I left him naked
Her resting at his feet like a sacrificial lamb
His tongue shoved deep in her snatch
His flaccid shriveled dick in her mouth
Rope removed, a note nailed to his chest
I missed a few times leaving embedded marks
Like the last one

THE RIVER

I went to the River to prey
To prey and study the land
To slink through the low lights
Slither closer
To the River
To prey

The Leader calls the sinners
Calls them forth to be
Washed from the light
To be washed in the River
They sing in the twilight
Calling to brothers and sisters
Lugubrious tones
To come from the light
Come sinners they call

I come
To the River to prey
The Leader wears red
His cloak stunning offensive
Floating on the River
Where he has come to prey
To bring them from the light
Into the Darkness
One by one
The sinners to Darkness
Come to the River
To be washed from the light

In death reborn to
Darkness' clutches
They are washed from the light
They float down River, down
Ghastly bouquets as they float
Through the doorless arches
That stands over the River
Where I came to prey

The corpses breathe
Splutter to life
As they pass the archway
That stands over the River
Where I came to prey

From Life to Death
To live once more
Reborn in the River
Where I no longer prey

THIRTY-TWO

Thirty two
They hang on the wall,
My collection of grisly souvenirs

The last barely a month old and showing little signs of decay.
This is my sanctuary, my quiet place, a space of reflection, where
I can be alone with those that know me best. Those that are a part
of me, their memories, their bodies, their minds.

The first is my favorite, my best, my love.

Her eye sockets are empty, the once vibrant colour gone,
leaving only a vacant stare.

I ate her.

Filleted her lean flesh from her bones,
and devoured her piecemeal over time.
She, like the others is a treasure box,
her skull holding not grey matter,
but a jar,
filled with portions of her puréed organs, and brain.

The walls are pristine white,

Were

The drippings and droolings of crimson mark each place.
I call it art, though some may disagree.
Insane?

Death By Poetry

We are animals, humans,
Given teeth in which to tear flesh from the bones of other animals.

Are you any different?
Do you not devour the blood and meat of animal life in order to survive? To feed yourselves?
Are you better than I?

Granted, my actions would be frowned upon in polite society
They call it cannibalism; I call it survival of the fittest.
I sit in judgement of the only ones who would dare to do so,
The only ones who matter.
The Devoured.
They who sacrificed their lives in order to feed me, albeit

But not my first, my heart.
She watched me suffer as I suppressed my desires,
choosing only to bite and not tear,
to draw blood and not drink,
sometimes shaking uncontrollably
with the paroxysms of passions.

Only then did she see the error of her ways, her thoughts,
and gave herself over as first meal to my strong jaws,
Smiling as I tore great chunks from her inner thighs, the rest. She
screamed joy at my release, begging and pleading

I punctured her eyes,
Sucking them from her head like some rare delicacy.
The release was too much for her,

the delicate flower that she was, her heart staggered it's last beats
like a trapped bird in a cage.

Ah memories.
You never forget the first, and she,

My fragile angel,

with hair like spun glass, tasted like spring.
Her blood reminiscent of early morning dew,
so much so that imbibed it like fine wine.

How her vitality danced on my tongue;
no other has come close.
They all taste tainted, spoiled somehow.
Perhaps this one will be different.

TOUJOURS

Who am I?
But one of many
Those who vie for thy attentions
Sweet as molten honey
Rich thy lips must be
I pine for just the slightest brushing
The tiniest sparkle of thy bejeweled gaze
Radiating love as thy loving hands
Enclose my tortured throat
Eyes collide
Toujours, mon cœur
I die

U – Y

UNAFRAID

On days when I grow quiet
Lost in my head
Tongue tied and twisted
The words just won't come
Unable to speak what screams in my heart
My mind a berserker, trapped in it's box
Rigged to explode, should clarity fail
.

When I'm alone on the edge, in rage or in darkness
You touch me in ways I can't comprehend
Your hand on my soul, calms the storm
Silences the demons, behind those locked doors
The walls crumble slowly, frozen in rust
Crevices caulked in heartache and dust

Defenses of steel, wrapped in barbed wire
Razors and blades
You walk through every one unscathed, unwounded,
Unafraid of what lies inside these halls,
Unfettered by leavings littering the floors
.

Leaving me more confused than before
Huddled in corner, nowhere to run
You drive away the shadows I use to camouflage myself.
Exposing the scars under the light
Words soothing as though they were not there
It's impossible to think, I don't understand, it doesn't make sense

How can a mirror show the same reflection?
Differing views of the same direction?

VISCERAL KISSES

I saw him today again

He should be peacefully resting
In the hospital bed where I left him
Sated and sedated,
A desire smeared smile on his face
And his arousal still at half mast
He said my name as I slid
My lips, dressed in red
Across his hardness as he slumbered
Face bruised and battered
Knuckles abraded, his hand flexed
Immersed, wound itself in my hair
Holding me down,
The pulsating heat filling my throat

He woke then, glittering resplendent
Eyes entrancing, never left mine
Just clung and tussled in the air
Visceral kisses

I could then taste passion, palpable
Physical, he growled my name
Mildly threatening, a smile
His teeth shone sharply in the dying light
Venomously curious, I crept closer
His hand still wrapped in my hair
His lips hard and teeth soft on my neck
Distracted, he too occupied to notice
My reach for the syringe,

My body trembled, breath gasping

I slid home the needle through flesh emptying the vial
I gave into the sensations
His tongue drawing letters on my skin
Arms locking me to him

Shiver, regret as he fell away
Pulling me with him, and I kissed him
Achingly slow, I felt him stiffen
Frightened slightly, and softened
When his face did,
That desire smeared smile made him beautiful
I left him there, not an hour ago, sated and sedated
I still taste him on my tongue and there he stands
In the Lamb of God T-shirt I bought him
For Christmas, and beat up jeans
Pointing to the one lighted window
In the building across the street.
Loud voices, a party

No one will hear you
My black winged angel

He whispers in my ear
He was right
So trusting are these killers
They open the door so easily
As easily as my stake slides

Into the eye of the first
A bullet in the forehead of the second

And her
Her, I will make suffer
I think as she grovels and begs
Hovering over the body of her man
I put her out of my misery
He calls me, hand out
My phone rings and I listen
Shiver, regret, I stand in front of the window
The lights shatter the night
The air is heavy and I float
The world flutters
His hand is warm in mine

WHAT IT'S ABOUT

It's about the fear
Your mind is not your own
It quibbles and nips at your will
Slowly stealing your fight
Until all that is left is a dream
A place you go when the hitting starts
Unrealistic visions of life without him
Life without menace or malice
Where Love isn't spelled P-A-I-N
It's about the long brutal silences
They drag, ad infinitum
Anxiety is the name of the game
Eyes travelling for the fiftieth time
Desperately trying to seize on IT
That thing that is causing the quiet
And you begin to pray for the explosion
Something to begin it so it can end
It's about the secrets
Interrogations and justifications
Desperate apologies, plaintive pleas
No one can know about the
Ribs, bruises, abrasions
Shhhhh. I'm sorry. .
Empty promise, never again
I love you.
Until the hammer falls again

That's what it's about.
It's about the fear, silence and secrets

WINTER'S MASK LIFTED

I sometimes wonder where I stand
How I stand at all and say terrible things
To myself
in my mind
Because to speak is too ugly
To close to the soul
And it's been marred too often
Bared too much to run and hide from a fight
I don't want to fight. Not anymore and
I'm too tired to try to be anything else
But what I am
Which was the point before I got too high
And distracted by the sound of snow melting
With the smell of spring lilting on the air
Like the delicate scent of lost flowers
That bloom on a grave
Winter's mask lifted, Just a beautiful lie,
That's where I stand.
I hate winter

WRITTEN EFFIGIES

Take my hand
Show me
Teach me

Teach me about things I've never known
Why butterflies have dust on their wings
Or Spontaneous combustion
Or why time flies when you are near

Tell me stories, about magical places
Wide open spaces. No bars or cages
Stories about your world and the people in it
Written effigies of the spoken word

Lie with me in the grass lush and green
And listen to the night birds sing
Their familiar refrain, as the crickets keep time
Your hand in mine, the worlds between us far,
Infinite distance, wish on a star, for what cannot be
I keep you in a heart shaped box, hidden from view,
And too, hidden in plain sight, hidden in shapes and colours,
Blood on the blade

Leave you will, you must, Time holds for no man,
My eyes close, and you are just simply illusion,
Not real, delusion.

Pray for Infinite slumber,
Respite from the things that bite, only to awaken again,
Pillow damp with unspent words.

YELLOW LINED SHEETS

I find myself sitting on the bench
Beside the path, where we used to run
and play as children, innocent and free
Where we grew love, planted it deep
In the soil of our souls, and pledged forever

Here, where we folded our vows
on yellow lined sheets
Stuffed in the cracks of the wood
Notes written in the burning blood of our passion

How we burned for life, then.
We were invincible, bulletproof, immortal
Human and fallible,
Simply meat sacks at Fate's Will but we didn't know it

I find myself sitting on the bench
Beside the path, where we used to run
As I do each year since you left me
Leaving my love on yellowed lined sheets

Buried in the soil, not of my soul
But in the ground
Where lilies of the valley grow
Where you lay, ashes to dust

I miss you

YOU'LL NEVER KNOW

You say you can't reach me and throw your hands in the air, exasperated, but I warned you, when we met that I was a tragedy of perfection and you laughed as though I had been joking.

I wasn't joking and now you act surprised when my edges show and humanity peeks from the cracks and fissures.

You'll never know because you cannot hear the memories that scream in the dark, as you slumber unaware.

You'll never know how I bite my pillow to hold back the terror filled rage that I wake to every morning at 1:13 am.

You'll never know how I wake alone in fear, my cheeks burning and aching or how I choke on the blood that my eyes bleed, swallow it back until my tongue is metallic with unspent emotion.

You'll never know how I stare into dead eyes night after night, my hands tacky with the blood that covers your faces.

How lucky for you.

That you can rest and fly in your dreams,
How lucky you are that you'll never know.

YOURS TRULY

The sun in the trees takes the chill edge off the morning
As I sit on my steps smoking a cigarette
Dressed in a parka and sandals
(Ooh la la)

I may not be the height of fashion
With hair by Pillow and Restless Sleep
But in this quiet moment
Alone in the sunlight
Birds chirping and twittering
I am just myself,
Beauty queen and star stunner
(Said with an eye roll if you please)

Truly though, as my cigarette dwindles
So does the darkness for a while
For now, the sunlight in the trees
The trash talk of my kids inside
Kinda makes me happy to be alive.

Melanie McCurdie is a Canadian based writer who resides in Calgary, Alberta. She is the Warrior Mom of two challenging boys, a wife, blogger with The Twisted Path Group, supporter of Independent Film and Publication, and a horror junkie with a taste for words, and bloodsauce.

Made in the USA
Lexington, KY
20 May 2019